15 Day Resell Rights P...

LEGAL NOTICE

The Publisher has strived to be as accurate and complete as possible in the creation of this report, notwithstanding the fact that he does not warrant or represent at any time that the contents within are accurate due to the rapidly changing nature of the Internet.

This book is a common sense guide to profiting from Resell Rights. In practical advice books, like anything else in life, there are no guarantees of income made. Readers are cautioned to reply on their own judgment about their individual circumstances to act accordingly.

This book is not intended for use as a source of legal, business, accounting or financial advice. All readers are advised to seek services of competent professionals in legal, business, accounting, and finance field.

Any perceived slights of specific people or organizations are unintentional.

This manual is written in Times New Roman for easy reading. You are encouraged to print this book.

YOUR RIGHTS TO RESELL THIS EBOOK:

Thank you for purchasing This eBook, My name is **David Zohar** and I am the owner and CEO of several successful online Businesses. You can grab a <u>FREE</u> copy of my comprehensive Internet Marketing Success Course now at:

http://www.EbkeZine.com

With your subscription, you will get this great **Mini Software Creator** software for <u>FREE</u>, and you will be able to create your own software products and sell them to your visitors.

Click <u>HERE</u> Now To Subscribe and Get Your Own *Mini Software Creator* Package.

If you ever need to contact me, you can do so at:
www.Netcustomercenter.com

Table of Contents

From My Keyboard

Dear Budding Reseller,

Hi and thank you for your wise investment in this 15 day, step-by-step Resell Rights profits manual.

In the coming pages, I intend for you to follow a detailed, step-by-step, day-by-day, proven Resell Rights plan I have laid out for you, which I have personally tested, done, and reap the results and profits from.

I will be showing you what to do to succeed online as a marketing reseller that the average reseller do not.

As I write this, I find it fascinating, in some instances. For one, it is a plan that almost anyone can follow – you don't have to be a rocket scientist or even attend college to understand and follow this plan. Hence what I have aptly called "blindly follow your way to proven Resell Rights blueprint".

Two, this plan is really over simplified, which I hazard a guess that most resellers overlook some of hidden gems covered in the 15 Day plan. I will be guiding you within the 15 Day plan in doing what the average reseller do not do, which is responsible for the cutting edge between those who succeed and those who do not.

Don't worry about the fact that there are thousands of resellers out there with the same product, because I remind you, too, that not everyone will do it right when it comes to reselling. You have gained an immediate edge over other resellers just having a copy of this manual in your hands!

There is hardly any guesswork and planning required on your part, because you will find them all right here, within the coming pages. I will also show you what and where to outsource for all the things you need to get started for under $200.

Be forewarned, though, that because your maximum investment is only as little as $200, this can spell investing more effort on your part.

Recommended Advice before Starting

While this is optional, I strongly recommend that you take a day or two off and rest from working on your Internet Business, if that is what you have been doing all these while.

Take a day or two off from your regular daytime job as well, if possible. If you cannot do that, at least take your weekend off and do nothing.

Don't think about your daytime job. Don't think about your boss. And no, don't even think about your Internet Business.

I hope you don't take this advice too lightly. If you have been working on something that has not been working for you all these while, it would not make any sense to continue doing so. A definition on *insanity* is one who does the **same** thing **over and over** again and expecting **different** results.

What you have been working has never brought any concrete results, so why should it bring any right now?

But if you take your mind off work for a while, you might just see what you had been missing out and not doing right in your initial plan with a better, refreshed mind!

Also, you will learn that the 15 Day Resell Rights profits plan which I have laid out for you in the coming pages are intensive in a way. While the good news is that there is no need for you to invest thousands of dollars in making old mistakes and even discovering new mistakes (that is quite costly), nothing would materiliaze if you do **NOTHING**.

You are probably all worked up by the time you read this, after trying many other things which are not working for you in your Internet Marketing career.

So I strongly urge you take a day or two off before starting. Take an evening stroll. Go for a jog in the nearest park. Visit the woods. Or take a short trip to nearest village or the bad side of town and realize how fortunate you really are – at least you have a working computer with an Internet connection.

My advice is not worth 2 cents – it can be responsible for your next explosive income.

With that said, it's **game time**.

Warm Regards,
David Zohar

Day 1

Firstly, here are a few assumptions I would make about you.

- You've got no previous experience in Internet Marketing.

- Even if you do have previous experience in Internet Marketing, they are probably not amusing and non-profitable. No offense intended when I say this, but wouldn't you opt for a better option which I am about to offer you?

- You don't know anyone online, not just yet.

- You are ready to start all over. You have got no web site, no auto responder, no web hosting, no Resell Rights products, and no anything.

And I would tailor this entire 15 Day Resell Rights plan with you being all of the above in mind.

Alright, let's kick-start the 15 Day plan today!

Now to be frank, your first day isn't going to be as amusing as you have initially thought, but it is probably the **most important** of all the 15 days covered in this plan. Ultimately, that is because what demand you will decide to cater to today will also decide the form of your next Resell Rights success!

So, what is on the plan today? **Start with what you know best**. It's work time – get a piece of paper and pen, and write down a list of 50 to 100 things you are good at or know a lot about.

Yes, I know this would demand some courage and confidence on your part but don't come up with mental excuses such as "I am not really good at anything". Personally, I think that is a sign of low self-esteem and in some extreme cases, it is stupid. When I hear comments like that, I often wonder, "If you are not good at anything, what the heck have you been doing for the last X number of years from the day you were born?!!"

So, write a list of **50 to 100** things you are good at or know a lot about. Write **more** than 100 things if you can.

Just to stimulate your thinking, check out the following suggestions:

- Are you good at dancing or sports?

- Do you know how to cook? Do you cook well?

- What are your hobbies? What do you do during your free time?

- Are you very experienced in your relationship with your partner/spouse?

- What topics interest you?

- Are you good at writing? What do you write?

- Do you like to read self-help books?

- Do you have any ideas you would like to sell to others?

- Are you good at fixing things?

- Are you a professional or consultant? Is there anything you can teach others about your profession?

Notice that I want you to begin with something you like or you are good at, because I firmly believe passion is the most important form of fuel that will keep you going before you start making your money.

Once you are done with your list of 50 to 100 things, take a 5 minute break. Review them shortly, and chose 10 of the 50 to 100 things in the list which you want to build your Internet Business on. Don't make bias decisions and don't worry if there any Resell Rights products available for them.

When you pick out your top 10 choices, go online and visit this URL:

http://inventory.overture.com/d/searchinventory/suggestion/

What you are going to do right now is **niche market research**. What I mean by this is that you want to meet a huge demand – real people with real money, who are willing to pay for something online.

So, run a quick search for keywords associated with your list of 10 things you are good at or know a lot about.

For instance, some of the things you are probably good at are:

- You are a relationship expert,

- You like collecting cans in your free time,

- You enjoy playing Tic Tac Toe (and a master at it, too!). *(Note: I know this sounds nutty but I have a point to demonstrate, just be patient!)*

We will start with can collecting first. Let's see if there is a niche for can collectors online.

I went to the URL above online and type in "collecting cans" in the Search box. After a few seconds, the results are found below (see screenshot):

Keyword Selector Tool

Not sure what search terms to bid on?
Enter a term related to your site and we will
show you:

- Related searches that include your term

- How many times that term was searched
on last month

Get suggestions for: (may take up to 30
seconds)

| collecting cans | ⊙ |

Note: All suggested search terms are subject
to our standard editorial review process.

Searches done in September 2005	
Count	**Search Term**
204	beer can collecting
45	can collecting

Quite simply, **the higher the count, the better**, as it indicates how often people use the keyword when searching online. (That means that there is quite a demand here!)

Unfortunately, in the case of can collecting, there are too few people who share the same passion as you in collecting cans. I doubt if there is any other way you can make a lot of money from can collecting, aside from selling them for cents to old truck that makes rounds around your neighborhood in search for recyclable items.

Now, let's try a search for "Tic Tac Toe". I have done this and the results are:

Keyword Selector Tool

Not sure what search terms to bid on?
Enter a term related to your site and we will
show you:

- Related searches that include your term

- Estimated number of times that term was
searched on last month

Get suggestions for: (may take up to 30
seconds)

| Tic Tac Toe | ▶ |

Note: All suggested search terms are subject
to our standard editorial review process.

Searches done in September 2005	
Count	Search Term
12576	tic tac toe
988	tic tac toe game
533	tic tac toe shoes
340	tic tac toe online
227	play tic tac toe
210	tic tac toe sock
207	java tic tac toe j2ee
156	free tic tac toe game
144	how to win tic tac toe
137	tic tac toe strategy
136	tic tac toe game board
121	3d tic tac toe
103	tic tac toe dance shoes
94	history of tic tac toe

That is quite a search here. The keyword "tic tac toe" was searched 12,576
times on one particular month. But can you **CAPITALIZE** on this niche?
Not a chance, either, even if the search figures go up to 6 figures.

If you think about it, there is no money to be made from this niche. I mean,
who on Earth would be willing to pay even a dollar on a step-by-step
champion strategy on how to win in a 3x3 tic tac toe game? I doubt if
anyone would want the manual for free, either.

Bottom-line: Just because there are plenty of searches for a particular keyword, it does not equate to money.

Now, let's check out how you can make money from your relationship expertise, particularly "dating". The following are the searches for "dating":

Keyword Selector Tool

Not sure what search terms to bid on?
Enter a term related to your site and we will show you:

● Related searches that include your term

● Estimated number of times that term was searched on last month

Get suggestions for: (may take up to 30 seconds)

| Dating | ▶ |

Note: All suggested search terms are subject to our standard editorial review process.

Searches done in September 2005	
Count	**Search Term**
5451133	dating
2242589	online dating
2017506	online dating louisville
1054633	adult dating
741594	online dating service
607847	dating site
564699	free online dating
558684	people relationship dating
376883	dating services
295521	free dating
198755	single dating
188554	internet dating
181551	christian dating
147282	dating web site

WHOA SH*T! 5,451,133 searches! That's 5.4 Million Plus!

If you are indeed a relationship expert, you have got a niche to capitalize on! The demand for dating is great, and people go online to search for information and services on dating in the masses.

It is obvious that there is a goldmine to take your share of gold from right here, but we are not really done yet. There are a lot of lonely singles on this planet who are looking for the "right partner", so much so that they are willing to pay for good information on how they can achieve this, or even pay to join services on matchmaking.

However, while the keyword "dating" brings 5.4 million plus searches, you have to be more "specialized".

In other words, you have to focus on a certain demand. This happen offline all the time. There are shops that specialize in repairing cars and there are those that specialize in repairing bikes.

Too little people have what it takes to create and run a turnkey or wholesome businesses like a chain of restaurants, shopping malls, and supermarkets, but everyone can start and run a specialized business, right?

That is what you are going to do in this case. Using the same "dating" case study, check out the other searches that people especially search for:

145451	christian dating service
112721	gay dating
73265	jewish dating
62756	dating personals
59778	lds dating
38717	senior dating
38245	asian dating
36273	black dating
36158	dating tip
34543	sex dating
32998	lesbian dating
32700	interracial dating
32657	indian dating
30129	free dating services
28816	dating lexington online
27736	dating advice
24394	hispanic dating service
24326	bbw dating
22221	speed dating
21253	latin dating
20570	online dating site
18048	dating personal
17183	dating chat
16365	dating agency
15933	free dating site
15458	dating services online
14998	dating game
13107	married dating

Perhaps you can start a business on giving "dating tips"? The keyword yields 36,158 searches. You can easily dispense dating tips in the form of articles or a short report, anyway – a lot easier than giving a dating service!

It pays to be more specific, though – how about dating for guys? I personally think that "dating tips" is still too general, but if you focus on "dating tips for guys", you know very well that your prospects are ALL guys, which sure is a dead certainty!

You want to be focused on "tips" because the truth is that you **cannot** be "everything". Not with only $200, you cannot! Let's face it: you cannot give online dating services, run a membership site, and write a series of eBooks on the subject in 15 days (probably take years, more money, and staff on salary).

But you sure can specialize in dating tips and reselling eBooks on dating, right?

Bottom-line: Decide on what niche you want to cater to today. This is where your business will be built on for the next 14 days and beyond. Yes, I know that ultimately, you want to resell products with Resell Rights. However, meeting the demand comes first, not the product. If people are not looking for the information found in the product, it cannot sell anyway.

Day 2

I trust that you have already researched your niche market and decided to tap onto it. Today, you are going to **write a series of 10 articles for your eZine**.

Step 1:   Decide the name and theme of your eZine

If you are in the dating niche, for example, you can dispense dating tips to your subscribers. Above all, provide free but useful information to your subscribers.

Give your eZine a name. For example, you can name your eZine "Jane's Dating Tips for Guys eZine". Your eZine has got a name, and the theme is clearly spelled out.

Step 2:   Write Your Thank You Letter

Your subscribers will be getting this letter immediately after subscribing to your eZine to confirm their free subscription. It can go like the following:

Subject: {First Name}, Your Subscription to Jane's Dating Tips eZine

Dear {First Name},

Thank you for your subscription. You are subscribed to my eZine as {First Name} {Last Name} at {Email}.

In case you have not received your free copy of my mini report just yet, you can download it from the link below:

{Download Link}

Please check out my first seductive issue on dating tips for guys like you tomorrow, {First Name}!

Warm Regards,
{Your Name}
{Domain Name}

Step 3: Write 10 Articles

Open your Word Program or Note Pad and write your articles. You will be using these articles to dispense information to your future subscribers on a weekly basis via your auto responder. These articles can be short stories, tips, strategies, personal insights, and so on.

Your articles need not be lengthy – 300 to 750 words each would do – as long as they are related to your niche market. This is too easy to do in a day.

*Important! Format your articles to 55 characters per line each, as if you do not follow this guideline, your Email letters would appear "jumbled" and "ugly" by the time it reaches your subscriber's Inbox. Also, make all fonts appear in Courier New, Size 10, as this is the standard text mail appearance for most mail programs out there on the Internet.

Again, if you are in the dating niche, for example, you can dispense dating tips to your subscribers. Above all, provide free but useful information to your subscribers.

Here is how you can format each of your articles:

Subject: {First Name}, {Insert Title Here}

Dear/Hi {First Name},

{Insert Article Body}

Until the next time, {First Name}!

Warm Regards,
{Your Name}
{Domain Name}

After you have written 10 articles, take an hour's break and return to review your articles. Proof-read and correct any parts of your articles where needed. You have to do this **only once**.

Bottom-line: Most resellers do not really take much priority in list-building. I think it is almost everything to an Internet Business owner of any kind, and it is an asset worth building, whether you have 100 or 100,000 people in your mailing list. Also, most resellers do not really have a "voice" or "control" of their own.

Although the idea of reselling other people's products is to skip the product creation process which can be time, effort and maybe money consuming and earning 100% of the profits for every copy of the product sold, it is important to have a degree of control yourself.

It WILL take some effort to achieve that, but it is effort worth investing.

Day 3

Today is going to be **very hectic** but be prepared for it – **write 30 articles**!!

Okay, I know this may sound insane but believe me that this actually very achievable. **No**, you are not going to write a 3-page essay per article, as if you are entering the exam hall to sit for your Physics test.

Each of your articles, again, does not have to be lengthy – 300 to 500 words would do, which adds to 12,000 to 15,000 words.

The articles should all be relevant to the theme of your chosen niche. Like the previous day, your articles must focus on providing free, useful information.

Using the same example again (I will be using "dating" as an example throughout the 15 Day plan, if you have not guessed, but you are free to choose your own niche market), write 30 articles on dating.

I trust you are an expert in this domain and that you have no problem writing. If you are good at writing, you will be able to complete all 30 articles in one day.

Now, if you facing some mental blockage, I have to remind you that there are quite a number of people out there who have written **more** than 30 articles in a day. **So can you**! After all, college students probably churn more than the amount of words mentioned above on an exam day, I do not see why this cannot be achieved, especially when you have definitely got a passion for what you are doing.

So, write 30 articles today. Get them all done and retire for the day.

If You Are Truly a Hopeless Writer

So, you do not dominate writing. Here are some suggestions on how you can get around accomplishing your 30 article challenge:

Get your articles written with the help of a friend or family member. Look for something in your 3 feet range now. That's right – it is going to be your family members and your phone line! If you are not a good writer, you can get some free help from your trusting friends or family members who can probably help proof-read your work or assist you on article writing.

Go to elance.com. This is going to cost you some money, but I would not be counting this into the $200 budget, as it is up to you to invest additional sum into hiring a capable ghostwriter from that web site. You can bid and hire a ghostwriter for at least $5 per 300-400 word article written. This can be time and effort saving – if you are ready to invest at least $150, that is.

Why 30 Articles?

You will discover why this is the case in the next few days of the plan. Also, if you are familiar with article writing, notice that I did not ask you to include your resource box just yet.

We will save that step for later on, as up until now, you have yet to get a domain name which you can call your Internet Business home.

Day 4

Create an 8 to 20 page free report of your own, which is relevant to your niche market, and appealing to your would-be subscribers. This report would be free for your subscribers to give away to other people in their network.

If you are wondering why you should write a free report of your own, here are the reasons:

☑ Most resellers do not have a "voice" of their own. While the idea of becoming a reseller is to skip the product creation phase and get into profits in the shortest time possible, but you might want to ask yourself: "Why should people buy from ME rather than from the principal product author, or other resellers?" You are going to make a stand-out here by having your own personality and control in your web site. You have gone through some tough article writing for the last two days and here you are again writing, this time your own report, but the truth is that if you do not do all these, you are no different from the other average resellers who are not willing to invest some additional effort and hence the average income.

☑ This report you will be writing is an upfront sign of "prove your worth". Having your own report in your name gives you a chance to prove your credibility and why people should trust your recommendations and advice in the first place.

☑ With the Internet completely awash with eZines, standing out of the crowd is more important than ever. Offering a copy of your free report is an incentive for subscribers to join your mailing list.

☑ If your subscribers like your report, they would give it away. Since you might not have what it takes to create a quality, paid product, you can always dispense free, general information your mini report, which can comprise of 8 to 20 pages. With your eReport being viral by nature, anyone who purchases anything from your built-in affiliate links in your eReport can result in bringing you back-end income! (More on that later)

Creating Your eReport, Step-by-Step

1. Open your Word Program, and create your front cover with a title. Don't worry if you do not have good designing skills, because your front cover be done simple and professionally like in the example below:

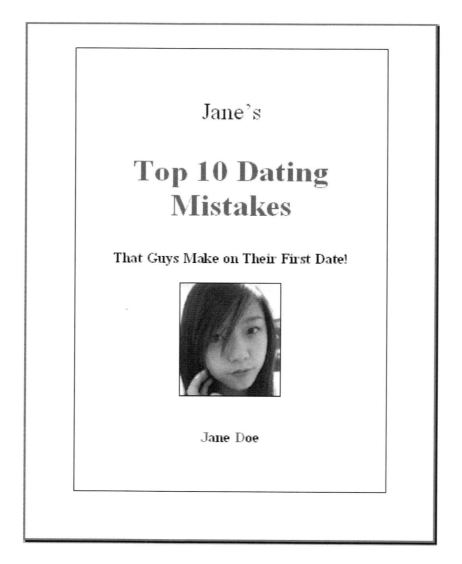

You can include any suitable images on your front eReport cover. It can even be a picture of you, too! Alternatively, you can source for copyright-free images at http://www.sxc.hu/.

2. Create **8 to 20** pages of content in your eReport. Since the pages are relatively short compared to any other eBooks out there, having your own Table of Contents page is optional.

Quick Tip 1: Remember the articles you have written for the last two days? You can squeeze, edit, mix, and match some of their contents into your eReport, which can result in saving you some time from creating your information content from scratch.

Quick Tip 2: If you need more content, a quick and free way you can use is to use articles with free reprint rights found at http://www.ezinearticles.com/. There are plenty of articles found in this article directory and they all have free reprint rights. You are allowed to use any articles of your choice to include in your short report as long as you include their author's resource box/bylines. You can pick and choose any articles you want from that article directory that demonstrates some of your points in your eReport.

Once you are done, take a break, and later review your copy to improve. Leave it in Word format for now. Retire for the day!

Day 5

It is already the 5th day of the program, and so far, all you have done is writing, writing and writing. There will be hardly any writing for you to do today, because first thing's first: get an account with PayPal at http://www.paypal.com/.

Registering for a PayPal account is free, and the one thing good about this merchant account is that the deduction rates are so low that they are negligible. At this time of writing, PayPal rates are **2.9% + $0.30.**

Once you have an account (and verify it) with PayPal, go to PayDotCom at http://paydotcom.com/. Registering an account with PayDotCom is free, too, as long as you have either a PayPal or StormPay account registered. There is an option where you can upgrade to Premier account for $29, but you do not need to do that as basically, you just want to join some useful affiliate programs that you can recommend in your 8 to 20 page eReport.

Cost of joining as an affiliate is zero, and this is a good way to earn some additional income simply by giving your eReport for free to your subscribers at your lead capture page!

Once you have registered with PayDotCom, look into the marketplace and search for affiliate programs to join. Find suitable ones which you can recommend in your eReport, and preferably that the affiliate program pays you on a recurring basis. Affiliate programs like these are likely to be in the form of membership sites and services.

After you have signed up for a few affiliate programs (3 to 4 will do), include all of your affiliate links in your eReport in the form of advertisements or recommendations to your reader.

When you are done with embedding affiliate links into your eReport, proof-read your work again. Leave your Word document the way it is for now as we will come back to that later.

PayPal Doesn't Support Your Country?

If PayPal does not offer withdrawal support and services in your country, you can opt to register for an account with StormPay, alternatively, at http://www.stormpay.com/. While registering for a StormPay account is free, you are required to verify your account to enable future withdrawals. StormPay will need you to register with NetIBA for $9.95 a year.

When you verify your account, it will take up to 1-2 weeks for the activation code letter to be mailed to your house, depending on where you live. The activation code is found in your mail, and you log into your StormPay account to verify it.

You can still use StormPay to accept your affiliate income from PayDotCom. However, do note that the deduction rates are really high, which is definitely a huge drawback for those who stay in countries not supported by PayPal.

Day 6

Today, you are going to create **3** simple, easy-to-do web pages for your coming soon web site.

Your Main Page (Index)

This is where all of your visitors should go to first when they visit your web site. So, open your HTML editor program and name your first web page file "index.htm".

The purpose of this page is none other than collecting your visitor's names and email addresses. There would be any hard selling on this page, well… not just yet!

So, how are you going to collect your visitor's details? How are you going MAKE them give willingly? Simple.

Remember the short eReport you have created the day before? You are going to give it away for free in exchange for their email addresses so you can follow up on your prospects later with your other offers which you will have in the near future.

You have probably guessed it by now where you are really heading – you are going to **build a mailing list** of your own, something which the average reseller would not bother to do with effort.

Here is a rough format of how your lead capture page can look like:

Insert Attention-Grabbing Headline Here

Insert Sub-headline here

From: **[Insert Your Name Here]**
Date: **[Today's Date]**

Dear Friend,

[Introduce yourself]

[Address your prospect]

[Introduce your free eReport]

[Sell your visitor on the benefits of your free eReport, neatly arranged in a table with bullet points]

[Gently remind your visitor that he or she will be subscribed to your mailing list and that he may unsubscribe at any time and his email address will not be shared with anyone]

[Insert Opt-in Form here]

Warm Regards,

[Insert Your Name Here]

In some instances, it looks like any other sales letter you read out there on the Internet but the fact is that if you do not sell your prospect on the benefits of getting a copy of your free eReport and subscribe to your mailing list even for no money down, **a freebie cannot even sell**.

Everything in your page should be completed except for the Opt-in form, which you will be getting an auto responder for this at a later time.

One Time Offer (OTO)

You can name this second web page file "oto.htm". This is where your prospects that opt into your mailing list from the initial page go to before downloading your free eReport. They will see this page where you give your "One Time Offer".

So, what is going to be in your One Time Offer? We have not really discussed anything much about you reselling products with Resell Rights up until now, but this is where you will be putting a group of "common-themed" Resell Rights products for your One Time Offer.

I will show you where you can high-quality, in-demand Resell Rights products in the truckloads later and that furthermore, many people have not probably seen them in the Internet marketplace, but that will come later. For now, create the frames of your One Time Offer page using your HTML Editor.

You can copy the example in the next page for your One Time Offer page:

Note: Leave your One Time Offer component blank for now. We will come to this part later.

Just before you download my eReport...

Check Out My One Time Offer Below!

Important! **Read the offer below – <u>very carefully</u> – as you will see this <u>only once</u>! Once you click away from this page, this offer will NOT be made available to you, *FOREVER*!**

(Insert Your One Time Offer Here)

Insert Headline

Insert Subheadline

This is where you include a group of high-quality Resell Rights products for offer!

☐ **Yes**, I would like to take advantage of this offer.

☐ **No, thanks**. I would have to pass this offer, knowing that this offer would not be made available to me again, ever. Now, please direct me to the download page where I can get a copy of your free report.

Thank You for Subscribing Page

You can name this web page file "thankyou.htm" or "tq.htm".

This is where you include the download link to your eReport for your prospects who have decided to pass on your offer and want to proceed to getting a copy of your free eReport.

Your Thank You page format can be like the following:

Thank You for Your Subscription

Please check your mailbox soon for your confirmation mail and first issue.

Mean while, you can download your copy of the eReport below:

[Insert download link]

Warm Regards,
[Insert Your Name Here]

Day 7

You will be making your first investment in getting a domain name and web hosting. You can get both of them at http://www.doteasy.com/. This is by far the best, cheapest option you can go for as you can get 100MB free web hosting, file upload manager (this is good for you especially if you do not have a FTP program), and the domain name fee is as low as $7.45 a year.

Sign up for an account with DotEasy, and select a suitable domain name you can call your business home. It has to be related to your niche. Using the same "dating" niche example, you can perhaps name your dot com business www.janedatingtips.com. Make your domain name short, related, and easy to remember.

Once you are done registering for a domain name and web hosting account with DotEasy, go back to your previously written eReport (which is still in .doc format), and your 30 articles.

Firstly, write a short resource box to be included at the bottom of each of your articles. Your resource box should not exceed 400 characters or exceed 5 lines (standard article directory regulations).

Quite simply, your resource box is a brief detail about yourself and this is where you can promote your business. eZine publishers and article directory webmasters do not like to accept "cloaked sales letter" articles. However, you can include a link to your domain name in your resource box.

An example of your resource box can be like:

```
==================================================
Jane Doe is a relationship expert with over 7 years of experience in
relationship counseling. Visit www.janedatingtips.com and get a free
copy of her eReport on "10 Dating Mistakes" and subscribe to her online
newsletter to receive her latest dating tips, methods and relationship
insights.
==================================================
```

Lines: 5
Characters: 290

Once you have included your resource box in each of your articles, include your domain name details and resource box (or About Author page) in your eReport, so you can gain some funneled targeted traffic from your readers.

Proof-read your eReport for the last time, and convert your .doc eReport into .pdf format using your Adobe PDF Converter program. Notice that everything in your eReport remains intact. The words are the same, the links are still clickable, and the colors are what they used to be. However, your document, now in PDF format, is locked.

Remember to disable the copying function before beginning the conversion process to prevent content thieves from conveniently copying your work. After that, upload your first file (the eReport in PDF format) onto web host server via FTP program or File Transfer Manager.

Day 8

You will be making two more very important investments today for your Internet Business.

Firstly, get an auto responder with broadcast feature account at http://www.norabots.com/. You need this to build your own mailing list and since it has a broadcast feature, you can easily send out your own mails and offers anytime you want, which is something a free auto responder does not have.

Register for an account with norabots.com for $9.97 a month. You can open unlimited number of auto responders with norabots.com, which is perfect, because eventually, you need to build at least two separate mailing list: one for your prospects, and the other for your customers, which you can conveniently follow up later to give more offers, perhaps at customer special price.

Yes, this is probably another thing that the average reseller does not do so take advantage of this loophole, and there's your own gold mine to go to anytime you want!

After you register for an auto responder account, upload your 10 articles which you have written on Day 2. This is where the 10 articles come in!

In your auto responder control panel, set for your first letter, the "Thank You for Your Subscription" Letter, to go out immediately upon your subscriber's subscription.

Next, set your second letter, your first of 10 articles, to go out on the next day – one day after your first letter. Subsequently, set the remaining 9 articles to be released to your subscribers on a weekly basis. In other words, set the 3rd article onwards on a 7-day interval. That should keep your subscribers fed with free information you can afford to let go for 9 to 10 weeks (but always make sure you have a way to profit from every of your article, such as including your recommendation or ad in the form a link of your own, your affiliate link).

Now, go back to your first created web page, the "index.htm" file you have made on Day 6, and paste the Opt-in form codes at the bottom of the page, and route it to direct your prospects to the "One Time Offer" page link. Your index and main page is now complete!

Alright, now that you are done with your auto responder and routing, what's next on the to-do list for today? Ah yes, you haven't acquired any products with Resell Rights, have you? Okay, go to http://www.digital-resale-rights.com/.

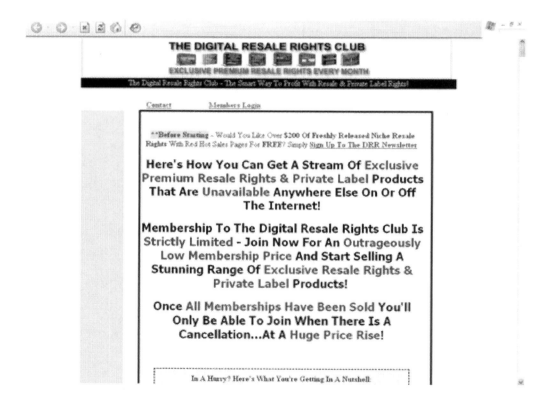

Exclusive, premium **Resale Rights** & Private Label Products, or so it the headline says. If you are into the dating niche, obviously the types of Resell Rights products you are looking are ***dating-related***. Since this is a membership site, we should be able to see what the owner of this site has to offer.

I scroll down the sales letter. So far, I get all the good stuff on what is in for me, but no trace of what he is offering inside his membership site yet... wait... I see it now!

Awesome! Just the collection of products with Resell Rights that you need! And apparently, the webmaster of this site adds quality products with Resell Rights from time to time.

It is obvious that he is capable of providing a variety of niche products with Resell Rights on a consistent basis rather than the usual Internet Marketing products that most other Resell Rights membership owners offer out there, making this an ideal membership site for you to join.

Check out what else he is offering:

<u>Recipe, Food & DrinkNiches</u>

The Complete Library Of Cooking (5 books of recipes)
100 Succulent Chinese Recipes
101 Camping & Outdoor Recipes
101 Recipes For The Deep Fryer
600 Recipes For Chilli Lovers
Cheesecake Recipes
470 Crock Pot Recipes
Chocolate Recipes For Chocolate Lovers
Delicious Diabetic Recipes
Delicious Italian Dishes
Great Sandwiches Volumes 1 & 2
Mouth Watering Apple Recipes
Fish Recipes
Delicious Puddings
<u>Delicious Soup Recipes</u>
Ice Cream Recipes
Quick And Easy Cooking: 155 Time Saving Recipes
The Appetizer Collection
Recipes From Around The World
The Big Book Of Cookies
Summer Party Cooking Recipes
Ultimate Chicken Wing Cookbook
300 Chicken Recipes
400 Refreshing Punch Recipes
Salad Recipes

Cool, another collection of niche products with Resell Rights! There are more in the list of products he is offering at his membership site as this is just one of them. By the way, food is a *hot* market, too! I mean, we all need to eat everyday, right?

Also, this membership site has a training center for all resellers so this is ideal for you, too, as a reseller. So, get a membership account with Digital Resale Rights club for $29 a month. That is a very unfair bargain for the webmaster, since you get to have everything for that low fee, which would definitely cost you more if you acquire the Resell Rights to the niche products individually.

Once you get an account with Digital Resale Rights, download all (and I mean literally ALL!) the products with Resell Rights that you need for your niche together with their Reseller Materials Packs and save them into your hard drive.

Ah, finally! You have acquired a collection of Resell Rights products! We will put turn them into assets tomorrow. And since you are subscribed to the membership site, you can enjoy the privilege of receiving updates and a collection of newly added products every month, on a consistent basis!

Tip: If are into the Internet Marketing niche, you will do well to resell the products by Digital Resale Rights club, as another benefit of being their member is that the affiliate links in Digital Resale Rights eBooks are rebranded to yours, enabling you to earn recurring income for every successful referral you make!

Day 9

You will be doing up your One Time Offer sales letter today. Don't worry if this is your first time writing your own sales copy, and trust me, this can be accomplished in a day – if you follow me closely on this.

Firstly, browse through your collection of products with Resell Rights you have downloaded yesterday from the Digital Resale Rights club member's area.

Hand-pick any combination of **5 to 10** products of your choice which you want to offer in your OTO page. Take note of their individual product pricing, write them down, and calculate their total amount.

Important! Check each product's Resell Rights terms and conditions to see if the original product author allows his or her product to be bundled in a paid package or sold as a bonus to another product you are selling.

Set a standard – be sure that the entire products with Resell Rights you are going to offer are not only high in quality but they are something that your customers can benefit from and use. Also, be sure that their total value exceeds at least $600.

You are going to sell the entire package at $67 to $97. This is the suitable range of pricing for a One Time Offer. Remember that your prospects will see this page first before downloading your free eReport, so make this an unusual, irresistible offer that he **CANNOT** find anywhere else.

So, go back to your half-done One Time Offer web page template and write your own sales copy in the One Time Offer component. Don't worry if this is your first sales copy, as I will give you a rough format guide you can easily follow, edit, mix and match, and adapt to.

Okay, here is something I think you should know – most principal product authors who provide Reseller packs for resellers to use usually give a pre-written or principal sales letter in their Reseller pack.

And very often, product authors allow their resellers to edit the sales letters, which is obviously a good thing for you, as in the case of writing your One Time Offer. This is because you can conveniently copy and paste (and do minor editing) the benefits of that product, together with other products, in your One Time Offer page!

Thus you **save time** on writing nearly half of your sales copy on your One Time Offer!

Alright, here is an example of how you can start addressing your prospect in your One Time Offer:

> *Dear Friend,*
>
> *Just before you get your hands on my eReport, I would like to bring up this One Time Offer to you, which I strongly think that you should consider. Don't worry, you can still get my eReport whether you accept or pass this offer, but please read this VERY CAREFULLY as you will see this letter ONLY ONCE!*
>
> *I know you are a busy individual, but I assure you won't be wasting your time reviewing this offer, here goes:*

A good way to start your letter, right? Continue your letter, confirming your prospect's problems/challenges and later introduce the all-in-one solution, which he probably could not find anywhere else.

This is where you introduce the products with Resell Rights, all lined up well, like in the example below:

Insert Product Title #1 (Worth $XX)

[Insert Product Benefits]

Insert Product Title #2 (Worth $XX)

[Insert Product Benefits]

Insert Product Title #3 (Worth $XX)

[Insert Product Benefits]   *… and so on!*

You can copy and paste the benefits from each product's individual sales letter all into one – your OTO page! Also, you can use the product's eCovers and images to give your prospect a nice look and impression, to encourage the making of the sale.

You can throw in some bonus products as an incentive for your prospect to take advantage of your offer right now, on the spot, if you want to. Summarize your letter by totaling the amount of products value and later pitch in that he can get all of the products worth $XXX for the price of $67 to $97.

It can't be any simpler! You don't really need to attend a copywriting course to know and do this, but you really do need to know how to tap onto your prospect's desire to get all the turnkey solutions and the idea that he can save so much time and money (and maybe pain as well!). That is, if he takes advantage of your offer on the spot **right now**.

Complete your sales letter, take an hour's rest, and return to it to proof-read it from the perspective of a prospect. Do some corrections where necessary and leave it as it is right now, since you will put it to the profits test it soon enough.

Day 10

Task 1: Create a Thank You Page

Create a Thank You page for your customers who purchase your One Time Offer special. Your customers will be redirected to this page to download both your free eReport and your offered products with Resell Rights.

Task 2: Create a Buy Button with your PayPal account

Now, go online and log into your PayPal account. Create a purchase button, set with your OTO product price and details. This is so your customers can pay you via credit card or PayPal money. PayPal is the Internet's most-used money broker online, so it would be wise to use PayPal to accept your customers' credit card transactions.

Later, copy and paste the code from your PayPal control panel into the bottom of your OTO sales letter, where your Order Button or Order Form is placed. Route it to the Thank You page URL where your customers can go to download the offered products with Resell Rights and your eReport after purchasing your package.

Once you are done with this, upload all of your files and products to your web host via the File Transfer Manager or your FTP program. Check everything to make sure they appear correctly and that the download links are working.

Your web site is up for business!

Task 3: Submit ALL of your articles!

Now, the promotion and marketing efforts begin, with all the setting up done (thank goodness, you have to do the setting up only once!).

Recall the 30 articles you have written on Day 3? Go to http://www.articlebar.com or http://www.ezinearticles.com/, and register for a basic account. It's free for registration, so get an account and submit your first article. Don't forget to include your resource box!

It would take one to a few days to get approved as an expert author. When that happens, submit the rest of your 29 articles at one go! The rational behind this is that you want to get as much exposure as possible. While there are several article directories out there, eZinearticles.com is one of the few web sites that provide the kind of heavy traffic you want.

Since there are plenty of traffic in this article directories and when you submit 29 articles at a go, not only would it make your articles more noticeable by visitors and eZine publishers, you can quickly achieve Platinum Author status.

From my personal observation, it takes 20 to 25 articles for an expert author to be upgraded to Platinum Quality author. That would be evident when you receive a star icon next to your name in every of your articles. But the reason I have pushed you to write 30 articles is so you can get a surefire guarantee you will achieve that kind of status.

I think that is important, because not only would readers take notice of your effort and seriousness in your business, you can almost bet that quite a sum of your readers would find out more about you through your web site's link in your resource box!

Now, that is where some of your initial traffic will come from, and how you can start building your mailing list from scratch – *cost free*! And since article directories like eZinearticles.com and articlebar.com receive high traffic daily, your articles can serve as an auto-pilot traffic funnel into your domain name's lead capture page where your Opt-in form is strategically placed!

Want Leverage? If you want to leverage your article submissions, you will surely want to try http://www.articlemarketer.com/. In a nutshell, Article Marketer, as the name itself is self explanatory; helps submit your same article to multiple eZine directories and publishers.

There are free and paid options that determine the amount of exposure your articles will receive. But if you are on a strict budget, the free option will do just fine, whereby your articles will be republished and reprinted by a limited number of eZine directories and publishers.

Day 11

With your setting up phase accomplished, it is time to build your mailing list – at **warp speed**.

Your article submissions have given you some upfront exposure, but that would not be enough, especially if you want to build your mailing list into **at least the 1,000** subscriber base range as early as possible.

Personally, I think it is important to achieve this minimum amount first, because if you have less than 1,000 subscribers in your mailing list, you will be handicapped of many benefits, privileges and options.

Firstly, if you want to participate in a Give Away venture, all of their webmasters would require each participating JV (Joint Venture) partner to have a minimum 1,000 subscriber mailing list. While you can say any amount of subscribers you have to the webmaster, more often than not, the results will show when you endorse your Give Away JV link to your subscribers – talk about giving away!

Secondly, when you achieve a minimum 1,000 subscriber mailing list, you can confidently sell advertising space in your eZine issues, if you want to. Okay, but you still need to start somewhere! So, you need to build your mailing list in the shortest time possible.

At this time, you should still have virtually <u>zero</u> subscribers count in your mailing list, as your article submissions just took off yesterday, and they take a day or two to be approved as this is probably your first time.

And since you have 0 in your mailing list, you cannot do an ad swap offer with anyone just yet. So, what is really left to do is – **buy subscribers**!

No, you are not going to buy bulk mails, which anyway, I am against that. But you can buy subscribers from World Wide List, where they display a list of eZines (like yours) and get in subscribers for you for cents per subscriber subscribed to your eZine as a result of their efforts.

Go to http://www.listbuilderpro.com/listbuilder/index.html. You will learn that a lot of people, including top Internet Marketers and Entrepreneurs whom among of them are probably those you follow after, endorse this service.

Register for an account with them and list your eZine details in the proper category. It takes up to 24 hours for them verify your account.

Make your eZine as attractive as possible in your eZine details. Don't pay more than 10 cents per subscriber. This would probably get you single opt-in subscribers but that would be enough. You can either double-confirm their subscriptions in your own eZine or cultivate your list from there.

Tip: In your eZine details, let your prospect know that he can get your free eReport.

While List Builder Pro offers a comprehensive quotation of their services, pick any single opt-in quotation that is below $60. That should fetch you 300 to 500 subscribers in a month. Remember to set your List Builder Pro account to accept subscribers at 10 cents or less. That would result in a lower listing in your category since the rates are based on bidding, but that would be fine for now.

Configure your List Builder Pro account so that your prospects enter your Lead Capture Page or your "mini sales letter". The logic behind this is that you want them to see your One Time Offer before getting their hands on your eReport.

If you write your sales letter compelling enough, and since your prospects are already well-targeted (provided you list your eZine in the right category), your sales letter should convert a minimum 2%. In other words, every 2 of 100 prospects who see your One Time Offer will buy from you.

And assuming you price your One Time Offer $67, you will earn **$134** per 100 subscribers subscribed to your eZine! Rope in 500 subscribers a month with List Builder Pro, and you can earn around **$670** – or even more! And as for those who did not buy from you on first contact, you can still follow up on them with other offers since they are subscribed to your mailing list!

I know that this sounds theoretical but in reality, a lot of people do earn more than that. There is little doubt that the success factors are:

1. Your sales letter. Write a compelling sales letter for your One Time Offer, and the conversion rates can be high, even more than 4%.

2. The kind of prospects you bring in. Bringing in targeted prospects is almost as crucial as writing your sales copy. Fortunately, as long as you list your eZine in the right category at List Builder Pro (a.k.a. World Wide List), you will get targeted subscribers.

Keep these in mind, and you will profit from your investment as you keep buying subscribers at the same low rate of less than $60 a month. The result: you earn upfront sales and build your mailing list at warp speed at the same time – **auto pilot**!

Day 12

Now that your mailing list building is in progress, you need to get reinforcements. I mean, **network reinforcements** – another thing that the average reseller does not bother investing in. Business is already tough, but don't do it alone!

Whatever products you sell, that makes you an Internet Marketer, ultimately, for whatever you sell using the Internet as a medium.

So, go to one of the most popular and highly-trafficked Internet Marketing forum online – the Warrior Forum. While there are many other forums dedicated to Internet Marketing, there are no forums that are quite like this, in my opinion.

Go to http://www.warriorforum.com/forum and register for a free account. And next, read the rules, not post your first post! You will quickly learn that like any other forums, this forum is against spam. I would hate to see you rush in with your first enthusiastic post that can read: "Hey, I'm a newbie. Check out my website at [insert whatever jibba-jabba link here]". Not only does it deserve to be deleted, it gives you a moron's impression.

Drop that, and post your first post in the main discussion forum by introducing yourself. Tell everyone here who you are, what you do, etc.

Don't:

1. Tell people how your marriage ended up in a divorce.

2. Reveal your age (especially if you are too young or too old).

3. Spam. Don't go asking people to click on your web site's link whatsoever. You can however, include your web site's link in your signature file.

4. Admit how much you lack in your Internet Marketing/Resell Rights knowledge. It is okay to be a beginner, but it is not okay to let people have that kind of bad impression of you. I think that giving yourself away that WAY is a bad impression that can last, since this manual is entitled 15 Day Resell Rights profits. I am not asking you to "fake it until you make it", either, but you can always shut up about it, right?

Bottom-line: First impression counts.

Do:

1. Introduce yourself.

2. Let people know who you are briefly. You might just pick up some new friends with the same common goals and interests.

3. Let people know what niche you are in. You can find potential partners in success without much guessing!

Bottom-line: Network with a healthy group of business associates who can help you with your business for mutual benefits.

After your first post, check out the other threads in the forum to participate and help out where possible (that is what forums are for). Make an effort to post at least once a day in effort to help, or even ask honest business questions. You will find yourself heading in the right track!

Why else come here? Aside from the above mentioned reasons, here are a few other benefits of coming here.

Firstly, when your list reaches an acceptable amount of subscribers, you can post ad swap request threads in the Joint Ventures forum.

Quite simply, you endorse other eZine publisher's ads to your list while the eZine publisher does the same for you to his list. Since the forum is frequented by savvy Internet Marketers, you will find some people interested in your offer contacting you.

Do ad swaps with as many eZine publishers as possible and you will find yourself with many subscribers in a short period of time, free of charge.

Also, when you submit your ads to eZine publishers who are interested in your offer, your ad should be compelled and written to endorse YOUR free eReport, not products with Resell Rights that you are selling whatsoever. Get them to your Lead Capture Page and when they opt into your form, they will see the One Time Offer.

Some will buy and some won't. And talking about those who buy, as long as your sales letter is compelling (converts 2% and above) and that you are swapping ads with eZine publishers who have the type of prospects you are looking for, you can make money simply by swapping ads literally!

And another benefit to name is that you can check out the Special Offers forum in search for products with Resell Rights that you can acquire at a deep discount or "unseen offer", simply by virtue you are a Warrior member!

When you need to reinvest in acquiring more "rare" Resell Rights products to resell to your subscribers, you can look no further than this forum and Digital Resale Rights membership club.

All in all, make it a ritual to post once a day at this forum – and invest some time in networking with your would-be business associates who can definitely help you in your future ventures.

Day 13

Two more days until the 15 day plan is up! Okay, the routine is getting clearer. You are focusing more on building your list and networking – two important things that most resellers either ignore or take too lightly.

Today, you are going to invest some pocket money into big time advertising. I say "pocket money" is because the fee is... well, let's just say you cannot afford NOT to afford it!

I am talking about those $7 to $15 offers that allow you to submit an ad to 100,000 over subscribers. I recommend http://www.mywizardads.com/ for this advertising purpose.

If you have not done this yet, write your advertisements out first – one for Solo Ad, and the other an Endorsement Letter.

Solo Ads are usually 4 to 5 lines, while Endorsement Letters are very much personal letters from you (or an eZine publisher) endorsing your stuff to subscribers.

For most of the eZine publisher's convenience, format your ads to 55 characters per line.

What are your ads about? They are none other than promoting your free eReport. Why your eReport, you ask? This is because you want to collect as many subscriber leads as possible. Yup, LIST-BUILDING again!

While many people do question the effectiveness and whether their products do get sold via "$7 for ad to 100,000 subscribers", do not waste your money (although it is little) on selling your product immediately – collect subscribers first! Even if your subscriber does not buy from your One Time

Offer, at least he or she is in your mailing list, which you can follow up with another offer that might just appeal to him or her in the near future. Or do you want to spend another $7 just to get to him or her again while he or she is subscribed to other people's eZine?

Important: Like any other advertising campaigns, it takes time to get noticed. You may not get the kind of exposure you are expecting for the first time so you have to be prepared for this possibility. The good news is that $7 to $15 is an investment you can afford to publicize your eReport and web site to a huge subscriber base (in the hundred thousands) more than once.

Day 14

With one of your guaranteed income source to come from your One Time Offer and that you are steadily building your mailing list, go back to the Digital Resale Rights club and search for products with Resell Rights that you can resell to your subscribers.

Check out for any updates where possible. Alternatively, you can source and acquire Resell Rights products at its cheapest and newly released at the Warrior's forum which you are a member of now.

The product you acquire must come complete with Reseller Materials Pack (must include compelling sales letter and thank you page, most importantly), enabling you to just set up the pages, order form and credit card payment processor. After that, send an endorsement letter to your subscribers in order to profit in the shortest time possible. Depending on the size of your list and how responsive they are, you can profit even within hours.

So, source for a quality product or two that you can safely endorse to your subscribers and make sure it is something they are looking for. If you are into the dating niche, resell products on relationships and dating to them. It would not make sense to resell a "pets" eBook to your list, since they did not subscribe to your eZine for that common interest in the first place, am I right?

Make this a ritual as you build your mailing list. It does not matter whether you have 100 or 1,000 subscribers in your mailing list right now – but it does matter that you endorse quality products you have acquired the Resell Rights to your subscribers, something they can find useful or helpful.

You will quickly learn that some people will just unsubscribe from your mailing list. That is perfectly fine actually, because you did not set out to entertain people with your eZine in the first place. You build your mailing list to **make money**. And you make money by giving your subscribers a better solution, may it be something that they can save time, save effort, save money, or even make money with.

Day 15 and Beyond

There you go!

Your activities on days 1 through 10 are one-off, which means that they have to be done **ONLY ONCE**. Whereas days 11 through 14 are a routine, which you can easily do for about half an hour a day and when you become more familiar with it, it only takes up to 10 to 15 minutes of your time a day.

By now, you have probably learned that this 15 day Resell Rights plan stresses on two very important, fundamental Internet Business aspects where most resellers neglect or ignore – list building and networking.

The following are things you should be actively doing all of the time for your Resell Rights business:

1. Keep building your list. Maintain your account with List Builder Pro to build your list at God speed (okay, so that sounds exaggerated) in the shortest time possible and buy advertising space from eZine ad offers like Wizard Ads from time to time, and you will surely get your subscribers in the truckloads around the clock.

    Another free, effective way you can resort to is ad swapping, a mailing list owner's game of "subscribers making subscribers". Keep doing this with as many mailing list owners as possible and you will have your subscriber base grow manifold *cost-free*.

    With the One Time Offer technique I have taught you earlier in this plan, you will make sales upfront each time you get subscribers! This is possible because every subscriber will go to your Lead Capture to opt into your form, and they will see your One Time Offer first before getting their hands on your free eReport on offer.

    Keep track and improve your One Time Offer's sales letter until no improvement can be made. You know that you can stop improving your sales letter's conversion rate the moment your sales letter produces a minimum **2% to 4 %** conversion rate – the higher, the better still.

2. As for those who did buy from you for the first time, you can still follow up with other offers.

   Having looked that you are subscribed to Digital Resale Rights club as a member, you can return to the membership site as and when or upon notification that new products are added. All you have to do is carefully pick and choose the products that appeal to your subscribers, set their sales letter and Thank You page up, and resell them to your mailing list – you can be in profit within hours!

Think about it. You spend only a total of $131.40 altogether. That is far less than the $200 budget.

Now, I would not say that you will make indeed make money as fast as 15 days, and perhaps if you are attempting to follow this plan for the first time from scratch, you might take more than the initial 15 day plan, give a few more days.

However, the **real** bottom-line of following this plan is that you finally build a business in the right direction that rewards you continuously as a reseller. I have laid the reseller's roadmap out for you and shown you the direction. Having said that, all you need now is the passion and drive to take action and succeed.

To Your Resell Rights Success!

Warm Regards,
David Zohar
www.EbkEzine.com

Printed in Great Britain
by Amazon